Wizard Cat

'Wizard Cat'
An original concept by Rebecca Lisle
© Rebecca Lisle

Illustrated by Lilia Miceli

Published by MAVERICK ARTS PUBLISHING LTD

Studio 11, City Business Centre, 6 Brighton Road,

Horsham, West Sussex, RH13 5BB

© Maverick Arts Publishing Limited November 2020

+44 (0)1403 256941

A CIP catalogue record for this book is available at the British Library.

ISBN 978-1-84886-727-7

www.maverickbooks.co.uk

This book is rated as: White Band (Guided Reading)

Wizard Cat

By Rebecca Lisle

Illustrated by Lilia Miceli

Chapter 1

It was hard to be a homeless cat in the rain and cold. Wilfred had walked many miles looking for shelter. At last he came to a palace.

'Perhaps there will be a cosy corner in here for me,' he thought. There was a notice on the gate:

WIZARD WANTED. APPLY WITHIN.

But Wilfred was too hungry and tired to read notices.

Inside, he smelt a delicious smell. He followed it to the Great Hall, where the king, the queen and the princess were eating their lunch. He sneaked under the table.

'Funky footwear, King,' he thought. 'Smart slippers, Queen. Tidy little toes, Princess...'

He ate all the scraps of food that fell on the floor. 'Mmm, lovely grub!'

"Have you found your pink silk slippers yet, Poppet?" the king asked the princess.

The princess shook her head.

"I'm not buying you another pair," said the queen. "You go through so many! Dancing and losing them, and I don't know what..."

"But I left them in my room!" cried Princess Poppet. "I know I did!"

"If only we had a wizard," the king said. "A wizard would find the missing slippers."

'Who needs slippers?' Wilfred thought as he tiptoed up the grand palace stairs. 'I don't!'

He looked in all the rooms. One bedroom was all pink and fluffy. He liked pink and fluffy! 'Well wash my whiskers! It's purrfect!'

There was even a perfect bed for Wilfred, full of tissue paper to play with. He settled down and soon fell asleep.

SQUEAK, SQUEAK!

Wilfred was awake in an instant. Mice!

He jumped out of the box. 'How dare mice be here? In a royal bedroom? I'll get you!'

Chapter 2

But the mice were nimble. They were fast. They hopped and leaped and scurried into their mouse hole before Wilfred could catch them.

Wilfred's whiskers were twanging and his tail was twitching as he peered into the mouse hole. There was something pink and fluffy in there. Was it a giant pink mouse? He put in his paw and pulled the pink thing out.

The mice squeaked at him: "Stop! That's our bed!" It wasn't a huge mouse; it was a small pair of pink silk slippers. Just then the princess came in.

"My slippers!" she cried. "Oh what a clever kitty you are!"

She scooped him up and carried him down to the king. 'I do like Princess Poppet', Wilfred thought, wrapping himself around her neck.

The king was amazed. "The cat found them? What a thing!" he said. "So intelligent: a wizard sort of cat! Do you think he saw the notice on the gate? Do you suppose he actually thinks he can be the Palace Wizard?"

"I don't know, but he's very cuddly," said the princess.

"Well, cat, you can stay and try out for the job," said the king. He put a small wizard's hat on the cat. "There you go! That might help. All wizards have pointy hats."

Wilfred didn't want the hat. He didn't really want to be a wizard. He wanted a bowl of cream. 'Still,' he thought, 'at least I have a place to stay.'

Chapter 3

Wilfred slept in the wizard's room. It was full of spell books and potions, but he had no idea what to do with any of them.

'I don't know how to be a wizard,' he thought.
'But I'll do any sort of magic I can to stay here.'
That night, when everyone was asleep, Wilfred
heard an odd noise. 'More mice?' he wondered.
'Not in *my* palace!'

He crept down the great staircase. He didn't
see any mice. He didn't see *anyone*; everyone
was asleep. 'I'll nip into the kitchen,' he
thought, 'and see if there's anything to eat.'

He found some crumbs of cheese and ate those. He found a scrap of bread and chewed that.

He found the cook's ball of knitting wool and fought that bravely, patting it here and there and rolling it around the floor.

Again, he heard a noise, a creeping and sneaking sort of sound.

The living room window was open and the long curtains were blowing in the breeze. In the moonlight, he caught sight of a huge spider. Quick as a flash, he raced up the curtain after it. He *loved* chasing spiders.

The spider spun out of his way on a thread, but

Wilfred raced after it and...
CRASH!

The curtain pole fell, the
curtains fell and Wilfred
fell – but not onto the
floor. Something
large wriggled
beneath him.

'That's a very big spider,' he thought for a moment and then the *thing* beneath him began to shout.

"Get off me! Let me go!"

'That's no spider!' thought Wilfred.

The noise had awoken the palace. The king rushed in. The guards pulled the curtain free. Wilfred had caught a burglar.

"Huh, caught by a pesky cat!" the burglar moaned.

"Well done, cat," the king said. "I think you'll make a fine wizard. I don't know what sort of magic you are using, but it is brilliant!"

'Cat magic,' thought Wilfred, purring.

"Here is a wizard cape, cat." And the king draped a silky cape around Wilfred. "All wizards have capes. Now you just need to do one more magnificent bit of magic and we'll make you the *Official* Palace Wizard."

'Very nice I'm sure,' thought Wilfred, 'but a gift of sardines would be even better.'

Chapter 4

"Call the wizard!"

"Where is the cat wizard?"

Wilfred was curled up on Poppet's bed.

'Oh no,' he thought. 'I was having such a lovely dream; I had a huge bowl of cream and five sardines swimming around in it...'

He didn't want to move at all.

But the king needed him.

The king was in the Great Hall with the queen and the cook.

"Ah, there you are," the king said. "I suppose you were very busy making potions and casting spells? Practising to become the Official Palace Wizard?"

Wilfred just smiled.

"I called for you because there's an imp in the palace."

'An *imp*?' Wilfred didn't like the sound of that.

"Yes," said the cook. "It's a terrible little thing! It's green and spiky. It's making the cakes flop, the milk go sour and the tomatoes turn blue!"

"You must catch it, cat," the king said. "That is your final task. If you succeed, I shall award you the Official Palace Wizard Wand."

Wilfred had no idea how to catch an imp but he went to the kitchen and sniffed around. There was definitely something odd in there: a weird smell... and the feeling of being watched.

'Just like a rat,' Wilfred thought. 'I don't like rats.'

He stretched out on the floor by the fire and was almost asleep when he saw a strawberry under the table. He began to play ball with it, patting it around. 'It is fun being a wizard,' Wilfred thought as he scooted around the kitchen. Next, he caught sight of a strand of spaghetti trailing off the table and he began to tap and tug at it... But this spaghetti tugged back!

Wilfred looked up. There was the imp, holding onto the other end! It was such a horrid-looking thing that Wilfred let go sharply. The imp toppled over and fell off the table. It landed with a bump and squeaked angrily; it sounded just like a mouse...

Wilfred didn't think; he pounced! The imp wriggled and squealed and kicked but Wilfred dug his claws in and held on tightly.

He carried the imp to the king in his jaws.

Chapter 5

"Marvellous work!" the king cried. "Quickly, put the nasty thing into that jar!"

Wilfred did as he said. The queen put the lid on. The imp was trapped. It shook its fist furiously at them.

"Have him sent back to the purple mountains," said

the queen. "That's where these little monsters come from."

"I'll be glad to see the back of it!" said the cook, and he took it away.

"We've never had such a wizard!" the king told Wilfred. "I now declare you the Official Palace Wizard. Here is the magic wand!"

Wilfred took the wand. He didn't want a wand, he wanted smoked salmon...

Wilfred went back to his room. He looked at himself in the mirror.

'I look like a wizard,' he thought. 'I have all the wizardy things I need to be a wizard...
I wonder...?'

He closed his eyes, waved his magic wand and when he opened his eyes, his spell had worked: a bowl of cream! Sardines! *And* smoked salmon!

'Well wash my whiskers! I *am* a wizard!'

The End

Book Bands for Guided Reading

The Institute of Education book banding system is a scale of colours that reflects the various levels of reading difficulty. The bands are assigned by taking into account the content, the language style, the layout and phonics. Word, phrase and sentence level work is also taken into consideration.

Maverick Early Readers are a bright, attractive range of books covering the pink to white bands. All of these books have been book banded for guided reading to the industry standard and edited by a leading educational consultant.

Pink
Red
Yellow
Blue
Green
Orange
Turquoise
Purple
Gold
White

To view the whole Maverick Readers scheme, visit our website at

www.maverickearlyreaders.com

Or scan the QR code above to view our scheme instantly!